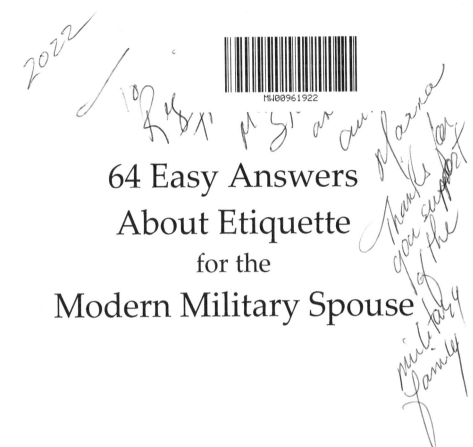

64 Easy Answers
About Etiquette
for the
Modern Military Spouse

Marna Ashburn Krajeski

This book is available at quantity discounts for bulk purchases.
For information, please call 401-487-2584

DEDICATION

To the guardians of courtesy and graciousness who believe,
as I do, that manners have a place in the 21st century

CONTENTS

INTRODUCTION

"Nothing is less important than which fork you use. Etiquette is the science of living. It embraces everything. It is ethics. It is honor."
Emily Post

In twenty years as an Army wife, I've committed the following social blunders: carried a drink through a receiving line; cancelled at the last minute; failed to RSVP to a wedding because there was no RSVP on the invitation (you're supposed to do it anyway); neglected to return hospitality and hurt a friend; displayed the flag without the union in the top left; and drank from someone else's water glass at a dinner party. If I'd had this handy guide, I could have spared myself some embarrassment.

The trouble with most etiquette manuals is they are lengthy and comprehensive. Who has time to absorb all the lessons from a three-hundred page book? Now there's a shortcut.

With *64 Easy Answers About Etiquette for the Modern Military Spouse*, you have a convenient guide at your fingertips. The frequently-asked-question format allows you to glance at the table of contents and consult the section you need, or read the book entirely in one sitting if that's your style. The information covers social etiquette and customs specific to military culture, such as what to do during reveille, retreat, and national anthems of foreign countries.

My book will give you a confident start for any situation. Even seasoned military spouses can benefit. Although I was an Army wife for two decades, I learned new things as I compiled this. While knowing what to expect in a military context can make you feel more prepared, remember the most important rules: relax, have fun, and enjoy yourself.

Marna Ashburn Krajeski

June 2012

OVERVIEW

1. What are etiquette and protocol?

Etiquette and protocol are basic good manners and common courtesies. They make you and others feel at ease and allow everyone to have a basic idea of what to expect in a given situation.

Etiquette – Etiquette represents good manners in daily life. It's not artificial behavior, but an accepted set of rules which help you to feel more comfortable in almost any occasion, and enable your guests to feel at ease when visiting your home.

In practical terms, etiquette means knowing the appropriate attire to wear to various events, how to act in certain situations, and what to bring for your host and/or hostess. More importantly, good etiquette is simply treating everyone graciously and respectfully, no matter their rank or standing in life.

Military Etiquette – Military Etiquette includes everyday good manners, along with the customs, courtesies, and traditions of the different services.

Protocol – Protocol lets us know what to expect in a military or diplomatic context. For most of us, it's a combination of military traditions, etiquette, and common sense. Knowing the guidelines will help you feel more comfortable. The installation Protocol Office is always a helpful resource.

2. What kind of social functions can I expect to attend in the military?

Brunch – This function is usually held around 11:00 a.m. and is a combination of breakfast and lunch. A simple dress, skirt and blouse, or nice pants outfit is appropriate.

Coffees – Unit coffees are usually held monthly and provide a wonderful opportunity to greet new arrivals, to farewell folks who are leaving, to become acquainted with other spouses in the unit, and to find out what is happening in the unit and on post. This is primarily a social outlet for the spouses. Refreshments are served. They may be plain or fancy depending on the host/hostess. Dress is usually casual.

Luncheons – Most Spouses' Clubs have a luncheon or similar activity each month. There may be a social hour before and a program after the luncheon. Reservations are almost always necessary. Membership in the organization is required to attend; however, many clubs allow you to attend your first luncheon before you have to join. A nice dress or pants suit is appropriate.

Teas – A tea is usually held in the afternoon and is the most formal of daytime functions. It is traditionally given in honor of a person such as a departing or incoming commander's or senior NCO's spouse. Coffee, tea, punch, cookies, and/or finger sandwiches are served. Expect to go through a receiving line and to sign a guest book when you first arrive. Wear a nice (Sunday) dress or a dressy suit.

Cocktail Parties – Cocktails are usually served from 5:00 p.m. or 6:00 p.m. until 7:00 p.m. or 8:00 p.m. They are usually about two hours long. Hors d'oeuvres or appetizers are served. The dress code is normally dressy dress for women and coat and tie for men unless special dress is requested on invitation (Texas casual, Aloha, Beach, etc.).

Open House – This literally means the home is open to guests between set hours. Guests are free to arrive and depart between those hours. Check the invitation for dress.

Buffets – A buffet supper is a dinner party served buffet style. It's a convenient way to serve guests, especially a number of guests in a limited space. At a buffet supper, the plates, silverware, napkins, and platters of food are arranged on the dining room table or buffet table, and guests serve themselves. Guests then find a comfortable place to sit as directed by host/ hostess. This kind of entertaining can range from fancy to barbecue style. Check your invitation for the required dress. Remember to wait for instructions from your host/hostess before going through the buffet line. The senior person present or the guest of honor is usually asked by the host/hostess to start the line.

Heavy hors d'oeuvres – Many times you will be invited to someone's home for "heavy hors d'oeuvres" which is very similar to the buffet dinner. There is no need to eat before you go. At these functions, a variety of foods such as dips, meats on small rolls, crudités, and desserts will be served. Dress should be indicated on your invitation and could range from casual to informal.

Seated Dinners – These dinners may range from the casual family-style to the very formal with place cards and many courses. Coffee may be served with dessert at the table or later in another room (living room). Check your invitation for dress.

3. What military functions can I expect to attend?

Promotion Party – A time-honored tradition is the promotion party that is given by an officer or NCO or a group of people with similar dates of rank, shortly after being promoted. It does not have to be a fancy affair, but it provides a chance to invite friends and their spouses to share the good fortune. You may also hear it termed a "Wetting Down." This is a Navy/Coast Guard term based on the tradition of pouring salt water over new stripes on the uniform to make them match the old tarnished ones.

Hail & Farewells (unit parties) – Unit members and guests share the cost and planning of these get-togethers. They range from dinners at local restaurants, to picnics and barbecues, to treasure hunts. This is a time to welcome incoming members and farewell members who are leaving the unit. These get-togethers build spirit and camaraderie, and they're a wonderful opportunity to get to know others in the unit.

Dining In – The Dining In is an old military tradition that has been passed down from the British. As the most formal of events, a Dining In allows officers and NCOs of a unit to celebrate unit successes and to enjoy its traditions and heritage. It is strictly an Officer/NCO affair. Spouses are not invited.

Dining Out – When spouses are invited to a Dining In, it becomes a Dining Out. This gives the spouses an opportunity to see all the "pomp and circumstance" that goes with the tradition. The spouse's dress is formal gowns or tuxedos.

Formals – Formal balls are usually held to celebrate special military occasions or a holiday. Proper dress is a formal gown or tuxedo. If Service Member is attending as a guest (not their own unit), then they may wear "spouse or guest" attire. On arrival, find your seats on seating chart. Mingle with the other guests. Visit with your host/hostess/special guest. At a formal or Dining Out, you will stand for the posting and retiring of the colors (bringing in and taking out of the flags). Stand for the invocation and toasts with the exception of the "to the ladies" toast (all ladies, including female soldiers, are seated) or "to the spouses" (female soldiers will remain standing and their spouse will be seated). There may be a receiving line. See Question #31 for information on receiving lines.

Receptions – A reception is usually held in honor of a special guest or guests, or after a change of command. There may or may not be a receiving line. Guests should mingle and visit with other guests. Before departing be sure to thank the hostess and host and bid good-bye to the guest of honor.

New Year's Day/Holiday Receptions – The long-standing Army tradition of a commander-hosted New Year's Reception for unit officers and their spouses, once a mandatory event in formal attire, has changed over the years. Many commanders choose to have

6

their reception on a day other than New Year's to allow people to travel, watch football, or spend time with family members.

The location can vary from the commander's home to the Club or Community Center. If held in their home, there may be a staggered arrival and departure time to accommodate a large number of guests. Don't be late and don't stay past your allotted departure time. No hostess gift is necessary as an official guest; however, a thank you note is a nice gesture. Check the invitation for appropriate attire, although it is usually "Informal." (See the attire chart in Question #5.)

Thanksgiving Dinner at the Dining Facility – This is a tradition to celebrate Thanksgiving together as a unit. Typically, the Dining Facility is beautifully decorated for the upcoming holiday season and Officers and NCOs dress in their service uniforms. Often there is a staggered schedule for large units. It's a great opportunity for unit fellowship as well as a reasonably priced full course holiday meal!

Parades – When you attend a parade, remember to be on time and dress appropriately. Children may attend if well-behaved. Take them from the immediate area if they are misbehaving. Don't bring any dogs except for seeing eye dogs. Remember to stand as the flag passes, and stand for the National Anthem, Division, and Service song.

Review and Change of Command or Change of Responsibility – The Change of Command is a ceremony in which a new commander assumes the authority and responsibility from the outgoing commander. You are welcome to attend a change of command ceremony without a specific invitation. However, be aware that attending the reception afterwards may require an invitation. If you're unsure, check with your senior spouse or representative.

Promotion and Award Ceremonies – These are significant events in the lives of the members involved and their families. As the presiding officer enters the room and is announced, everyone should stand. Later in the ceremony, as the award citation or promotion order is read, the announcement of "Attention to Orders" will be made. All military members stand at attention; civilians should stand out of courtesy.

Retirement Ceremonies – These ceremonies may be held with or without an accompanying parade or review. You are to rise when the presiding officer enters and is announced. As with promotions and awards, if Attention to Orders (the reading of the retirement orders) is announced, active duty will rise. Out of courtesy, civilians should as well. For all other portions, remain seated. Children may be welcome depending upon the formality of the event. There may be a reception afterwards. If not, it is customary for the audience to line up to walk by the retiree and spouse to shake hands and offer a few words.

Memorials – There are two types of Memorials—Service and Ceremony. A Memorial Service is religiously oriented and is voluntary because of its religious affiliation. A Memorial Ceremony is a command program with a ceremonial program and attendance may be mandatory for Service Members. Each installation and their command will decide whether or not to have memorials for their fallen heroes. You will be informed by the senior spouse or the chain of command how the command has chosen to honor the fallen. If the command allows memorials, it will also decide when and where. Dress according the solemnity of the occasion; therefore dress attire is categorized as "Informal." This means: Service Uniform with four-in-hand tie and appropriate "church wear." (See the attire guidance in Question #5.)

Spouse Welcomes and Farewells – Spouses of senior military personnel in the higher unit command are traditionally welcomed and farewelled separately from the Unit Hail and Farewell. The formality of the event will depend on how it's been done in the past within that unit as well as what the desires of the honoree are. Usually, they are held within the two weeks after the Change of Command unless there are extenuating circumstances like taking command during a deployment or during the summer months.

The reason a Tea or Coffee is recommended as a Welcome is to allow the Guest of Honor to circulate. A farewell function need not always be a Tea or Coffee. It could be a Brunch, Luncheon, or Dinner based on the preference of the Guest of Honor. There will probably still be a receiving line and guest book to sign and dress would still be "informal." The outgoing spouse does not usually attend a Welcome for an incoming spouse. Consult the incoming or outgoing command spouse as to their desires for when, what type of event, and how formal.

Send-off Ceremony – This is typically a ceremony on the parade field, or in the gymnasium if inclement weather, prior to a unit's deployment. It enables family members, community members, and other active duty people to see the deploying unit one last time before they leave and to wish them well. It is usually very meaningful and children are welcome to attend.

4. As a spouse, am I required to attend the social events?

No, you aren't required to attend the social events, but if you go, you might find them fun, interesting, and a good way to meet people. Friendships formed at these functions will unite you more closely with the other spouses, which is especially important should the unit deploy.

ATTIRE

5. How do I know what to wear to different functions?

Guests often wonder what to wear to a specific function. When you are in doubt what to wear, don't hesitate to clear up any questions when you call to RSVP. It's better to find out ahead of time than be sorry when you get there.

Always err on the side of being more nicely and respectfully dressed. The Five W's can help when deciding on the most appropriate attire for an event.

- WHO is hosting the event? Best friend and/or neighbor or the commander?

- WHAT is the event? A barbecue or a ball?

- WHEN is it? Generally the later the function, the dressier the affair.

- WHERE is it? Coffee at the bowling alley or at the club?

- WHY are we gathering? To make crafts for the bazaar or to honor the commander's spouse?

Invitations should have "Dress" in the bottom right-hand corner. It's important to learn the meaning of the dress terms commonly used in military social circles. The term "informal" is often misunderstood to be sports or easy attire. In fact, informal dress calls for a service uniform or coat and tie for men and an afternoon dress for women. Be familiar with these general guidelines:

Formal—Service Member wears evening dress uniform/dress mess. A female spouse or guest wears a long or short formal dress while males wear a tuxedo or suit w/bow tie.

Informal or Semi-Formal—Service Member wears service uniform with four-in-hand tie or equivalent. Female spouse wears nice dress or suit. Male spouse wears dark business suit. Note: If Service Member is attending as a guest (not their own unit), then they may wear "spouse or guest" attire.

Coat and Tie/Business—Service Member wears service uniform with four-in-hand tie or equivalent. Female spouse wears dress, suit, or skirt and blouse, but not as dressy as informal. Males spouse wears business suit or sport coat and tie.

Duty Uniform—Combat Uniform or Flight Suits (depending on the uniform for that particular workday). Spouse wears slacks or skirt and blouse.

Casual—Females wear a simple dress, skirt and blouse, or dress slacks. Males wear slacks and open neck shirt (no tie) and sport coat or sweater. No jeans.

Very Casual—Jeans, shorts, t-shirts (that are appropriate in nature).

Spouse Event—It depends on local customs and the time of day. For coffees, a simple dress, skirt, or slacks and blouse/sweater for females; slacks and shirt for males. Luncheons usually call for a dress, suit, or skirt and blouse. Traditionally, teas are the dressiest daytime function, so you'd choose a dressy suit or dress for females, or a business suit for males.

Marna Ashburn Krajeski

RSVP

6. What does "RSVP" on an invitation mean?

When you see RSVP on an invitation, it's an abbreviation for a French phrase which means "Respond please" and requires a yes or no answer. Respond promptly, within 48 hours, if possible. Accept with enthusiasm or regretfully decline. No explanation or excuse is necessary.

Answer by phone or in writing. Don't respond in person during an incidental meeting. The hosts may forget if you tell them at the Exchange or commissary where it can't be noted.

Even if an invitation doesn't contain "RSVP," it's still a good idea to make contact and inform the host/hostess of your plans to attend.

7. What does "RSVP/Regrets" mean?

"RSVP/Regrets only," "Regrets Only," or "RSVP/Regrets" all mean call only if you <u>cannot</u> attend. If you don't call, the host/hostess assumes you'll attend.

8. How soon should I RSVP?

Respond promptly, within 48 hours, if possible. The hosts need to know how many people will attend so they can shop accordingly, or add more guests if there is enough room.

Invitations may have an "RSVP by" or "RSVP NLT" ("no later than") followed by a date. This is the absolute latest you should wait to reply. Again, a prompt response is preferable.

It's a good idea to tape the invitation in a conspicuous place if you cannot RSVP when you open it. Write a reminder in your day planner so you won't forget later. Put the address, phone number, and time on your calendar.

9. What if I'm not sure if can attend?

Contact is imperative, whether your response is yes, no, or unsure. If you have another pending or contingent obligation which influences whether you can attend, call the hosts within 48 hours to regret and explain the situation. They will then have the option to accept your response or extend your deadline. The decision is up to the host.

Always remember to follow up and call back with a firm response later if you get the RSVP date extended.

10. Is it okay to ask if I can bring house guests to the party?

No. Only the names of the people written on the invitation are invited. If you are invited to an occasion and have houseguests, you may explain to the hosts that this is the reason for declining the invitation. This allows the hosts the opportunity to invite your guests, if they desire. Never ask if you may bring extra guests; the host will do the inviting.

11. Can I bring my children to a party?

No children, unless specified. Do not ask if you may bring your children. If you cannot leave your child/children at home with a babysitter or neighbor, then send your regrets.

12. I responded "Yes," and now I can't make it. What should I do?

Call the hosts or email them as soon as you realize you'll be unable to make it, not at the last minute.

Changing an RSVP to "Regret" should be for emergencies or illness only, and never because you got a better offer or you're too tired to make it. In all situations, it's best to keep the hosts informed.

13. My plans changed and I can make it, but I already responded "No." What should I do?

Depending on how close it is to the event and the type of occasion, you may call the host/hostess and explain the change in your schedule. Ask if it wouldn't be too inconvenient to change your RSVP to a "Yes" after the response date. A host/hostess may be able to accommodate a last-minute change if it's a buffet or a cocktail party; less likely if it's a sit-down dinner. Be understanding.

14. What should I do if I'm hosting an event and hardly anyone has sent an RSVP?

It's appropriate to call the invitees. A gracious way to handle this is to telephone the people who haven't responded, and after some small talk, mention, "I couldn't remember if you said you were coming to the party on Saturday or not." Remember to be kind about it. There could be extenuating circumstances, or perhaps they never received the invitation.

If there are too many people to call, ask the person in charge of the email roster to send out an email blast reminding people of the date and time and to RSVP. Often invitations have gotten lost in the confusion of daily life and a reminder is all it takes.

Marna Ashburn Krajeski

BASIC SOCIAL COURTESIES

15. What time should I arrive at a social function?

Come as close as possible to the time indicated on the invitation. Be on time or slightly late (10 minutes), but never arrive early. Call ahead if you want to come early and help, but only do this if you're close friends with the hosts. Wait until the invitation time to ring the doorbell.

16. What if I'm going to be late to a social function?

If you have to be more than ten minutes late, call the hosts to let them know. Call as soon as you realize you'll be late, rather than waiting until the last minute. The few minutes prior to start time can be hectic for the hosts.

17. What should I do when I arrive at a social occasion?

Remove your coat and find a place for it. Greet the host and hostess; greet the guest of honor, and then greet the senior ranking person.

18. What should I do before I leave a social event?

Traditionally, at official functions the senior ranking person leaves first. This is not necessarily true today; check to find out what is acceptable. If in doubt, wait.

- Do not leave immediately after dinner (wait at least 30 minutes to be polite).
- Do not overstay a welcome.
- Say "Good-night" to the senior person, the guest of honor, and the host/hostess.
- When you say you are leaving, leave. Don't linger at the door.

19. I never learned table manners, and I feel uncomfortable at social dinners. What should I do?

An eager student can easily and quickly learn table manners by observing and researching the rules in an etiquette book. A handy resource is *The Little Book of Etiquette* by Sheila M. Long. A more comprehensive book you may eventually want to purchase is *Etiquette* by Peggy Post.

It takes practice before manners become easy and automatic, but with determination and persistence, you'll pick them up. When in doubt, watch your hosts and follow their lead.

Here are a few simple rules to keep in mind:

- Take your napkin off the table, unfold it, and place it in your lap when the host/hostess does. This is usually after you sit down and grace is spoken.
- Generally, you use the flatware placed on the outside first and work inward with each course. When in doubt, take your cue from the host/hostess.
- Sit erect but comfortably. Take small portions and eat slowly.
- Don't talk with your mouth full.
- Chew with your mouth closed. Don't smack your lips.
- Keep your elbows off the table.
- Don't reach across the table to get something. Ask that it be passed to you.

- Spoon soup away from you in the bowl and then bring it to your lips.

- Use your bread plate. Break off a piece of bread or roll and butter each piece before eating. Never cut the roll in half and spread butter over all of it.

- When food must be cut, eat each bite before cutting another.

- Use the "OK Sign Trick" to determine your bread plate and drink. When you form the OK sign with your left hand, it makes the letter "b." This is the side for your bread plate. Likewise, the right hand "OK sign" makes the lowercase "d" for your drink side. This can be very handy at crowded tables when the place settings are close together. (Note: Do this discreetly in your lap.)

- When you are finished with your meal, place your knife and fork (with the blade facing the fork) on your plate at the "10 and 4 o'clock position." This signals your intention that the plate can be cleared.

20. What is a proper table setting?

For an excellent detailed explanation of place settings, see *Service Etiquette 4th Ed.* by Oretha D. Swartz.

This is a diagram for a formal place setting. At a less formal table, there may not be a soup bowl or soup spoon. Just one wine glass may be present at each place.

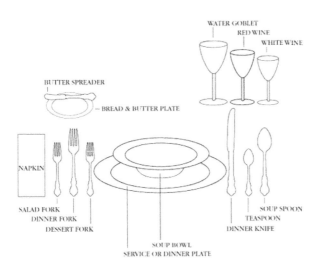

21. Is it okay to smoke at social functions?

It is not appropriate to smoke indoors unless the hosts allow it. Chewing gum and texting or talking on cell phones are generally frowned on as well.

22. Do I have to reciprocate when we've socialized at someone's house?

When you accept an invitation, it's kind and courteous to return the hospitality. It isn't necessary to host a seated dinner for a seated dinner. If you want, you can scale it down to "Appetizers and Drinks" or "Dessert Night" or a brunch, all of which are easier to do than a full dinner. Do what is comfortable for you and fits your budget. Paper plates, red Solo cups, and plastic flatware are fine. The important thing is the intent in your heart.

Don't hesitate to reciprocate hospitality from a commander or higher ranking individual. They'll be happy to get to know you in any setting. Over the years, each military family develops a personal style of entertaining. Your "picnic in the backyard with the kids" will not fall short.

INVITATIONS

23. I'm hosting an event. What should I include on the invitation?

Invitations can be formal, informal, or casual. They may be extended by written note, email, in person, by telephone, or sent through distribution. Only the names of the people on the invitation are invited.

Invitations should always include this information in the main body

- Date (day of the week and date)
- Time (if formal, write out the time, for example, ten o'clock)
- Place (where it will be held). Include an address that a GPS would recognize.

27

- Host/Hostess (if husband/wife -- informal: Bob and Carol Smith, formal: LTC and Mrs. Robert Smith, if unit: 407th Forward Support Battalion)

Bottom left corner of the invitation

- RSVP and mode of response: (you can use RSVP or Regrets only) with telephone number
- Cost: Under the RSVP of the invitation (if there is a cost associated with the function)

Bottom right corner of the invitation

- Attire: (casual, informal, semi-formal, formal, or specific dress guidelines, such as theme, i.e., Backyard BBQ or California Casual.) See attire guidance in Question #5.
- Extra notes: These might include "No cameras permitted," Gift table for the recipients of the function, etc.

24. When should I send invitations?

You should always send out invitations two to three weeks in advance. Four or more weeks in advance is advisable for very special or holiday events. For a major event, you may send a "Please reserve this date" card three to four months in advance.

25. What else do I need to know about invitations?

- Use black ink

- Avoid initials and abbreviations. Exceptions: Mr., Mrs., Dr., RSVP, or Captain J. Paul Doe (if an initial is used in place of a first or middle name)

- Write full titles, ranks, and names. Example: Major, Colonel, etc. In the Army, both First Lieutenant and Second Lieutenant are referred to as "Lieutenant."

- You may use "General" instead of Lieutenant General, etc. when addressing him/her.

- Dates and hours are spelled out on formal invitations with only the day of the week and the month capitalized. Example: Thursday, the eighth of May; "seven-thirty" is correct; "half after seven" (also correct) is more formal

26. What are the proper forms of address for formal invitations?

For more detailed information, two excellent resources are *Protocol* by McCaffree and Innis and *Honor and Respect* by Hickey.

The military member being invited in an official capacity is listed first:

> Major Mary Jane Doe and Colonel John Doe
> or
> Major Mary Jane Doe
> and Colonel John Doe

When both military members are invited in an official capacity, the higher rank goes first:

> Captain John Doe and Lieutenant Jane Doe
> or
> Captain John Doe
> and Lieutenant Jane Doe

Female military member and civilian husband:

> Major Mary Jane Doe and Mr. John Doe
> or
> Major Mary Jane Doe
> and Mr. John Doe

If wife is civilian and retained her maiden name:

> Captain John Doe and Ms. Jane Smith
> or
> Captain John Doe
> and Ms. Jane Smith

Military members are both of the same rank:

The Captains John and Jane Doe
   or
Captain Jane Doe
and Captain John Doe

Retired: Colonel Robert W. Thompson, USAF, Retired

Divorced from husband: Mrs. Jane Doe

Widow: Mrs. John Doe

27. Is it okay to send invitations by email or e-invitation services?

Hard copy invitations are always correct and proper. Receiving a hard copy invitation in the US mail shows effort and forethought. This tradition may be more appreciated by older generations. Often "Save the Date" emails can be sent out prior to the hard copy. In our changing world, however, electronic invitations and correspondence are becoming more and more common. Electronic invitations are often sent by email, via an attachment, or through a website such as Evite.com, Paperlesspost.com, or for official use, the Air Force's e-invitations.com (AFIT). Email invitations require the same response as any other invitation.

Things to consider before sending out electronic invitations:

- Your social group should get a consensus (all agree) that sending out information and invitations via emails or other electronic means is appropriate with the group.

- Be sure you do a test email so you are aware that all members are included and their addresses are correct.

- Blind Carbon Copy (BCC) members so their addresses are not visible to other group members/invitees.

- Depending on the function/occasion, a good rule of thumb is to send the invitation to the spouses two levels up and one level down.

- Spouses of Service Members, as well as the Service Members, should receive the invitation electronically if they are included in the invitation.

Advantages of Electronic Invitations:

- Getting information or invitations out is instantaneous; no waiting for the postal service.
- Easy and convenient
- Cost-efficient— no stationery or postage costs

Disadvantages of Electronic Invitations:

- Some people may not use email or have good access to email if they do not have a computer or internet in their home.
- Email addresses may be incorrect or misspelled.
- Email may go into the group member/invitee's spam folder without your or their knowledge.
- Some email addresses, like AKO (Army Knowledge Online), often strip attachments from emails, or can't be used with evite.com.
- Some computer systems are not compatible, so downloading attachments, invitations, or flyers is impossible.

28. Can I ask my spouse to deliver invitations via the active duty people?

This is a risky way to do it because with several middlemen, there are many chances for it to get misplaced or forgotten. If you're determined to do it this way, emphasize to your Service Member the importance of timely delivery. Invitations printed on colored paper, i.e. hot pink or lime green, will stand out and minimize the chances of getting lost in the white paper avalanche at work. An email follow-up to invitees is also a good idea.

CALLING CARDS

29. What are calling cards?

A calling card is a small card with your name on it, used in making visits.

Sizes—In the past, social calls dictated the size of calling cards for men and women.

- Married non-military woman's card is 3 1/8 inches long and 2 ½ inches high.

- The military man or military woman's card is narrower: 3 ¼ inches long and 1 5/8 inches high (traditionally it was narrower so it could fit in the man's jacket pocket).

- Joint cards: 3 ½ long x 2 ½ inches high.

- Most printers know the appropriate sizes, or your local Exchange can help you design and print a set of calling cards.

Mrs. Robert James Freeman

Robert James Freeman

Lieutenant Colonel
United States Army

Examples of traditionally worded calling
cards for spouse (above) and active duty
member (below).

Wording and Appearance—White paper with black printing is best for calling cards.

- Never use initials. Spell everything out, even the middle name.

- Rank should be spelled out in full. First and Second Lieutenants are simply "Lieutenant."

- On joint cards, rank may be abbreviated if the full rank and name would make the line too long

- "Junior" may be abbreviated to "Jr." if it makes the line too long. When written out, use the lower case j (junior) and when abbreviated, use a capital J (Jr.). Separate junior or Jr. from the surname with a comma.

- Use Roman numerals for "III" and "IV" and separate from the surname with a comma.

- Wives use their husband's full name preceded by "Mrs." and not their own first name.

- Wives who retain their maiden name may use calling cards with their name and no title or the title of "Ms." or their professional title if they have one.

- Chaplains' cards do not show their rank.

- For specific sizes and wording, refer to *Protocol* by McCaffree and Innis

Joint Cards—If you and your spouse decide to have calling cards made, you may order individual cards for both of you, as well as joint cards. If the spouse orders individual calling cards, her or she can order a large quantity because the information won't change. The military member will have to re-order calling cards after each promotion, so purchase these in limited quantity. Joint cards must be changed with every promotion and are less practical since their primary use today is for gift enclosures.

Lieutenant and Mrs. Robert Freeman

Example of traditionally worded joint calling card.

Envelopes—Envelopes are not used with calling cards left for social occasions. You may wish to order envelopes to fit the calling cards so you can use your calling card as a gift enclosure. Rarely, you may want to send a calling card through the mail, but if you do, you must enclose the card and envelope in a US Postal Service minimum size envelope (3.5 x 5).

30. When do you use calling cards?

Formerly, there was a rigid system of etiquette governing official and social calls. Social calls are no longer such a big part of everyday life. Occasionally, you will see a silver tray on someone's hall table in which to place your calling card. These days, the two occasions you might leave your calling card are at a New Year's reception held in the commander's residence, and the first time you are entertained in the commander's home.

At any base, post, or station where calls are still being made, you leave cards. Some commanders retain the tradition and prefer their officers and non-commissioned officers to leave cards. The Service Member can check with the adjutant or aide for guidance.

Conventional Wisdom—The number of calling cards to leave may have lost its meaning over time, but it's helpful to understand the traditional guidelines.

- A man leaves one card for every adult male and female of the host's household (including household guests), up to a maximum of three cards.

- A woman leaves one card for every adult female in the host's house (but never for a man) up to a maximum of three cards.

- A female in the military, invited because of her military position and not as the wife of her husband, uses the same formula as a gentleman.

- Joint cards are not used for social calls.

- A husband usually carries his and his wife's cards and leaves them either on arrival or departure.

- Calling cards are left (plain, not in an envelope) on a table near the door, in a small tray if one is provided.

Contemporary Practices—Though no longer a social necessity, calling cards are making a comeback because of their accompanying graciousness and courtesy. In modern times, calling cards have versatile uses:

- As gift enclosures—line through printed name and sign your first name.

- As informal party invitations—line through printed name and fill in information.

- As reminders—personalize with a note.

- As bearers of messages of condolence or congratulations.

- As acceptance or regrets to informal events.

- As a way to exchange contact information or change-of-address.

Messages on Cards—Messages in the form of initials can be written in the lower left corner of the top card (in pencil if the card is delivered in person or in ink if the cards are mailed). These are the traditional abbreviations associated with calling cards.

Initials	Meaning
p.p.c	*pour prendre congé* ("to take leave, to say goodbye") This indicates one is leaving the station or country.
p.p.	*pour presenter* ("to present, to introduce") This means that the friend who left the card is introducing a stranger to whom the receiver should send cards, phone, or call on. The stranger's name is written on the card.
p.f.	*pour feliciter* ("to congratulate")
p.c.	*pour condoléance* ("to extend sympathy")
p.r.	*pour remercier* ("to thank") To reply to a p.f. card.
p.f.n.a.	*Nouvel An* ("Happy New Year")
p.m.	*pour memoire* ("to remind") For example, to follow up on a telephone invitation.
n.b.	*nota bene* ("note well") To call attention to a written message on card.

Cards Can Also Be Folded to Signify a Message

- A folded top left corner means the visitor came in person; this corner unfolded means a servant was sent.

- A folded bottom left corner signifies a farewell.

- A folded top right corner means congratulations.

- A folded bottom right corner expresses condolence

Marna Ashburn Krajeski

RECEIVING LINES

31. What's a receiving line?

A receiving line is an efficient and gracious way to allow the honored guest to meet all the guests personally.

Those in the receiving line include: honored guest or guests, guest speaker, and host/hostess. If there is a red carpet, the receiving line stands on the carpet. Guests then go "through" the receiving line meeting each person.

32. What's the proper way to go through a receiving line?

Don't carry a drink or anything else through the receiving line. Place cigarettes, drinks, cell phones, headgear, large purses, and gloves elsewhere while going through the line. Often, there will be a small table before you get to the reception area to put your food or drinks on. If you can discretely hold an evening purse in your left hand or in the crook of your left arm, you may keep it with you, although it is preferred that you place your purse at your seat.

- The woman precedes the man through the receiving line at Army, Marine Corps, and Coast Guard functions. Sponsors precede their spouses or dates at the White House, Navy, and Air Force functions.

- The first person in the receiving line is the announcer, usually the Aide or Adjutant. You do not shake hands because the announcer isn't part of the official receiving line.

- The service member gives the announcer his or her rank and last name as well as his or her spouse's or guest's first and last name. For example: Captain and Mrs. Jane Smith. Out of courtesy, it's a good idea to provide your name even if you know the announcer.

- The announcer will pass the name to the first person in the receiving line.

- Exchange greetings and shake hands with each person as you move down the line.

- Repeat your name to members of the receiving line if your name hasn't been passed down. Speak clearly.

- Move through the line efficiently. You don't want to be the one causing delays in the receiving line.

33. What do I do if I'm part of a receiving line?

If you are a part of a receiving line, you should

- Be unencumbered of purses, gloves, hats, etc.

- Discretely keep a glass of water on a small table behind you.

- Wear comfortable shoes and don't lock your knees.

- Shake hands, make eye contact, and a exchange a brief greeting with each guest coming through the line.

- Repeat the name of the guest to the next person in the receiving line.

Marna Ashburn Krajeski

HOSTESS GIFTS

34. What is a hostess gift? Do I have to bring one?

A small hostess gift is always appreciated when visiting someone's home. It sends the message that you appreciate the invitation and the effort. This does not have to be expensive. Here are some examples of hostess gifts:

- Homemade cookies, muffins, or breads
- A local area delicacy
- Jellies
- A scented candle
- A bottle of wine (Be sure your host/hostess drinks wine and consider their preference.)
- A beautifully wrapped box of chocolates
- Flowers or a small plant

Include a card, a calling card, or note with the gift so the hostess knows who brought it.

If you bring flowers, don't present a cellophane-wrapped bouquet which requires your busy hostess to stop what she's doing and hunt for an appropriate vase. It's more considerate to bring flowers which are already in a vase. If you really want to bring loose stems, stop by earlier in the day and present them so she can arrange them as part of her preparation.

Your host or hostess might want to share your thoughtfulness of an edible gift or wine by sharing it with the guests. Consider this a compliment. Conversely, the hosts may put it aside for their own use later. It's their decision.

If possible, the hostess may try to look at the gift during the event and say thank you; however, thank you notes for a hostess gift are not required.

For command-sponsored events such as receptions and formals, a hostess gift isn't necessary.

35. If someone brings me a hostess gift, should I send a thank-you note?

Thank-you notes for a hostess gift aren't required, but you can't go wrong if you send a note or an email expressing your appreciation for the thoughtful gift and telling them how nice it was to see them at your house.

36. Does bringing a hostess gift take the place of a thank-you note?

No. While hostess gifts are a thoughtful gesture, it's good manners to send a personal note after the occasion. For assistance on writing a thank-you note, see Question #46.

Marna Ashburn Krajeski

INTRODUCTIONS AND NAMES

37. What's the proper way to make introductions?

There are guidelines about making introductions, but the most important thing to do is to make the introduction. Don't get seized up worrying if you can do it correctly.

When introducing two people, one is usually considered to take precedence over the other because of age, sex, or position. The honored persons name is stated first. The basic rules for introductions are:

- **Woman's name first.** Men are introduced to women by stating the woman's name first. "Sue Randolph, I'd like you to meet John Johnson." The exceptions to this are when the man is president of any country, a king, or a dignitary of the church, or when a junior ranking woman is officially presented to a senior ranking male.

- **Older person's name first.** Younger people are introduced to older people. When two people are of the same sex, the younger adult is introduced to the older adult by stating the older person's name first. "Mrs. Green, I'd like to introduce my daughter, Julie."

- **Senior officer's name first before a junior ranking person's name.** Junior officers are introduced to senior officers by stating the senior officer's name first. "Captain Jones, this is Staff Sergeant Wilson."

Apply common sense if two people you're introducing are in the same category. If it's a military setting, rank takes precedence. If it's a purely social setting, the importance of the female prevails. Remember Rule #1—Make the introduction.

Use first and last names when introducing people.

It helps to offer a bit of identifying information when you're introducing people, such as "Jane is my next-door neighbor."

If you are being introduced, respond with a smile and a handshake and a phrase such as "Pleased to meet you." Repeating their name will help you remember it.

When someone introduces himself or herself to you, respond similarly and include your own name.

38. Should I introduce myself to a senior officer or senior officer's spouse?

It is gracious rather than presumptuous to introduce yourself to a senior officer or senior officer's spouse. You should never be reluctant to speak to a senior person, although never monopolize the senior guest. Likewise, never be reluctant to talk with a junior person, making him/her feel welcome.

39. What do I call a senior spouse?

You should always address senior officers and their spouses by rank and last name (e.g., Colonel Smith) if they are active duty, or Mr./Mrs. Smith if civilian, until they ask you to do otherwise. Do not call them by their first names unless they invite you to do so. If you are asked to use a first name, it's polite to do so.

40. What should I do if I recognize someone but I don't remember his or her name?

The best thing to do is come clean right away. Don't try to fake your way through it. Mention that you recognize them or remember meeting them and politely ask for their name again. For instance, you might say, "We met at the Wilson's cookout. Can you remind me of your name again?" Give them your name as well. Chances are, they might not remember your name either. Get the names straight right away because the longer you wait, the more awkward it becomes.

If you are nervous about introducing someone because you forgot his or her name, politely ask for the person to repeat his/her name. This is certainly not a reason to avoid conversation.

41. We meet a lot of people. What's the best way to remember names?

Remembering names can be difficult, especially if you meet many new people in a short time. The technique can improve with practice. The first thing is to be fully present and give your undivided attention to the introduction. Shake hands and look them in the face. Repeat the name, "Cindy, it's nice to meet you." This will help reinforce the introduction.

A simple memory aid is to connect the new person/new name with something you already know. For example, when you meet someone named Nancy, you think "I have an aunt named Nancy and she has brown hair like this Nancy," or "Dan, like Lieutenant Dan from Forrest Gump, and this guy is a lieutenant too." It sounds crazy, but it works. Try it!

42. Where should I put my name tag?

Name tags are worn on the right side (the side with which you shake hands.) This makes it easy for the person shaking hands to look at your name. Right-handed people often want to place it on the left side, so be aware of this natural tendency and correct yourself.

Marna Ashburn Krajeski

TOASTS

43. What should I do during toasts?

The age-old custom of toasting remains an integral part of military occasions.

The mechanics of toasting are:

- Stand to participate in the toasting.

- Lift your glass and repeat the toast, e.g. "To the President," and take a sip.

- Those who abstain from alcohol may drink water or raise the wine glass without taking a sip.

- Never drink a toast to yourself; if seated, remain seated.

- All toasting is initiated by the host, except at dining-ins.

- At casual affairs, toasts may be presented by anyone.

44. I don't drink. Do I have to participate in toasts?

Yes, you can still participate in toasts by raising your water glass, or you may raise the wine glass in toast, but rather than drink from it, simply set it back on the table.

45. Should I drink a toast to myself?

Never drink a toast to yourself. If seated, remain seated.

THANK-YOU NOTES

46. What is a thank-you note and when should I send one?

A personal thank-you is always appreciated. It should be written within a week after you've been a guest at some occasion, been a houseguest, or received a gift. Rule of thumb: If you eat or drink at someone's home, or at their expense, say "thank you." Official command functions such as New Year's Day receptions and special occasions such as Hail & Farewells, weddings, and promotion parties are exceptions.

Promptness is important, but it's never too late to thank anyone. Try to get in the habit of writing a thank-you before you go to bed the same night. A stash of note cards and stamps kept in a handy place makes the task simple. Simple note cards you get at the stationery store are sufficient.

Address thank-you notes to the hostess only. Sign it from yourself. If you are writing as a couple, refer to the other person in the note. Example: "John and I had such a great time." Never sign a note with your spouse's name, too.

Here are the essential elements of a thank-you note:

- Thank you for (the name of the event or gift), and a short sentence expressing appreciation for being remembered.

- A sincere comment or descriptive sentence or two praising the delicious meal, the gracious hospitality, or the gift.

- A thanks again, mentioning the evening, dinner, gift, etc. and a request to be remembered to the host.

Sample of a Thank-You Note

Dear Mrs. Hunt,

Thank you for the lovely dinner at your home last week. The food was delicious, and I enjoyed getting to know the other guests.

Since we just moved here, it was especially nice to meet some new friends and to hear their helpful information about schools and attractions in the local area.

Thank you again for including us in such a wonderful evening, and please share my appreciation with Colonel Hunt.

Sincerely, Sue Jones

Remember, your expression of appreciation and promptness are what really matter, not how well you follow the rules.

47. Can I send someone an email thank-you?

Thank-you notes sent via email lack the personal touch of a handwritten card. Your hosts will appreciate the effort of a handwritten personal note. It's an enduring and thoughtful act.

Marna Ashburn Krajeski

MILITARY PROTOCOL

48. I'm new to service life and I don't know the military ranks and insignia. What should I do?

Make an effort to learn them, and learn them fast. There's no way around this. Find a chart of rank insignia on the internet or in the appropriate service reference books available at the Clothing Sales Store, the Exchange, or the installation library. Make flash cards. Ask your military spouse to quiz you at home or as you walk around the post/base. You'll need to learn not only the correct form of address (Sergeant, Corporal, Lieutenant) but the progression of ranks, i.e., which rank is higher, which has less rank. If you put your mind to it, learning them won't take long and you'll feel very comfortable in a short amount of time.

49. What should I expect at the gate when entering a Military Installation?

- When entering or leaving an installation with a guarded gate at night, dim your headlights 50 feet before the gate so you will not temporarily blind the gate guard.

- If you or a guest does not have a military ID Card, you will be asked to provide a picture ID.

- If your car does not have a Department of Defense (DOD) sticker and the driver does not have a military ID Card, you may be directed to the Visitors Station to register. Alternatively, you may be asked to go to the search area to provide your driver's license, car registration, and proof of insurance. You will be asked to get out of the vehicle, open all doors, trunks, and engine compartments, and step to the side while your car is searched.

- Even with a DOD sticker, you are still subject to random searches.

- Although speed limits vary on posts of different sizes, it's important to note that the speed limit in residential areas is 15 mph.

50. What should I do when the National Anthem is played?

You should stand quietly for the National Anthem.

When outside, place your hand on your heart and face the flag. Inside, you can either place your hand over your heart, have your hands at your sides, or behind your back. Civilian gentlemen should remove headgear in both cases. Outside rules apply if the ceremony is moved indoors because of weather or security. This may be noted in the program or by the announcer.

Don't talk, smoke, eat, chew gum, drink, use your cell phone, read, or otherwise occupy yourself while the anthem is playing.

Although not required, depending upon the solemnity of the occasion, it's appropriate to sing along.

51. What should I do when the national anthems of other countries are played?

It is respectful to stand for foreign country anthems but do not salute foreign flags.

52. Which songs require me to stand?

- The National Anthem

- National Anthems of Foreign Countries (do not salute)

- Reveille—The bugle call which marks the raising of the flag. See Question #57.

- Retreat—The bugle call marking the lowering of the flag. See Question #58.

- Ruffles and Flourishes—A tune about eight notes long that's played after "Attention" is sounded. When a General is present at an official event, the band plays "Ruffles and Flourishes" one time for each star the senior General in attendance wears. You should stand when you hear the first note.

- Official Service Songs—stand for your branch of service
    o *The Caisson Song* (US Army)
    o *Anchors Aweigh* (US Navy)
    o *Off We Go Into the Wild Blue Yonder* (US Air Force)
    o *The Marines' Hymn* (US Marine Corps)
    o *Semper Paradus* (US Coast Guard)

In addition, it's customary to stand at the following times:

- During the *Pledge of Allegiance*
- When the Colors Pass in Review

53. What should I do when the flag passes at parades?

You should stand when the colors are six paces to your right, in front of you, and for the six paces to your left, then you may sit.

54. What are Service Banners?

Service Banners, sometimes called **Blue Star Flags**, have long been a part of our wartime history. They are a way for households to indicate they have family members in the service. The blue star is placed on a white background with a red border. If a family has more than one person in the Armed Service, as many as five stars can be put on the same banner below one another. Department of Defense regulations permit the display of these banners during a period of war or hostilities. The Service Member doesn't have to be deployed in order for the flag to be displayed.

Blue Star Flag

The **Silver Star Flag and Banner** are symbols of remembrance and honor for those wounded or incurring illnesses during combat while honorably serving in the United States Armed Forces. It may be displayed or flown at anytime, not just wartime, and by families as well as the wounded and ill Service Members. The Silver Star Service Flag may be flown by anyone in remembrance of our wounded, ill, and dying during peace or wartime. This banner was added after the Iraq conflict.

A **Gold Star Banner** represents a Soldier who has died serving his country. When a Soldier dies in action, the blue star is replaced with a gold star. Another method is to put a smaller gold star on top of the blue star so the blue still surrounds the gold. These banners are usually hung inside a window; however there are full-size service star banner flags now available. If you decide to hang a full flag with a service star, it should be hung on the left side of your home. Therefore, when viewed from the street, you would see your service star flag on the right side and your American Flag on the left side of your home.

Service banners can be purchased through the American Legion (http://emblem.legion.org/Banners/products/873/). They are also available at CVS Flags (http://www.cvsflags.com/bluestar.cfm).

55. What is a Gold Star pin?

The Gold Star Lapel Pin was established by Congress in 1965 to identify widows, parents, and next-of-kin of Service Members killed in combat.

The Next-of-Kin pin signifies a service-related death or suicide during Active Duty other than combat. For example, a death during training.

When you see someone wearing a Gold Star pin or Next-of-Kin pin, it's appropriate to acknowledge it with words of condolence, such as "I'm very sorry for your loss."

Gold Star pin (left) and Next-of-Kin pin (right)

56. What is the Medal of Honor?

The Medal of Honor is the highest military decoration awarded by the United States government. It is bestowed on a member of the United States Armed Forces who distinguishes himself or herself "conspicuously by gallantry and intrepidity at the risk of his life above and beyond the call of duty while engaged in an action against an enemy of the United States."

The wearer of this medal is held in the highest regard, and all ranks salute a recipient, regardless of the recipient's rank. Additionally, wearers of the Medal of Honor are always saluted before others. Medal of Honor recipients are presented their own flag as well. You can find a complete list of awardees at http://www.cmohs.org.

The Medal of Honor

MILITARY SONGS AND HONORS

57. What is Reveille and what should I do when I hear it?

"Reveille" (rev ə lē) is a bugle call at 6:00 a.m. or 6:30 a.m. (times vary by installation) marking the raising of the flag and the beginning of the workday. If outside during Reveille, stand quietly at attention facing the flag or music with hand over heart or salute if in uniform.

On an Army post, if in the car and will not impede traffic or be unsafe, you should get out and stand. If there are children, remain in the car or use your judgment based on their ages.

On Navy and Air Force bases you are only required to stop and remain seated in the car.

Children should also stop playing and observe the custom of the ceremony.

When inside, stand with your hands at your side.

58. What is Retreat and what should I do when I hear it?

"Retreat" is a bugle call usually sounded at 5:00 p.m. or when the flag is lowered to mark the official end of the workday. It is followed by the bugle call "To the Colors," during which the flag is carefully folded and stored. Often a cannon will sound in between these two calls.

On an Army post, if in the car and will not impede traffic or be unsafe, you should get out and stand. If there are children, remain in the car or use your judgment based on their ages.

On Navy and Air Force bases you are only required to stop and remain seated in the car.

Children should also stop playing and observe the custom of the ceremony.

When inside, stand with your hands at your side.

59. What is Taps?

Of all the military bugle calls, *Taps* is the most recognizable and able to evoke emotion. The call is sounded at the completion of a military funeral ceremony. *Taps* is also played on an installation at 11 p.m. to signal the end of the day, when everyone is to go to sleep.

MILITARY FUNERALS

60. What can I expect at a military funeral?

The military funeral is a solemn and moving tradition based on customs developed through the years. All military members are entitled to simple honors, which includes a military chaplain to conduct the service and a flag to cover the casket. At the cemetery, a firing party fires three volleys after the chaplain reads the committal service. A bugler sounds "Taps," then the flag is folded and presented to the next-of-kin.

Top non-commissioned officers and all officers are authorized full honors, which also includes the use of a caisson (a two-wheeled wagon) or other modified military vehicle, pallbearers, an escort commander, a color guard, troops, and a band.

As with most funerals, it's a good idea to bring a handkerchief or a packet of tissues for the inevitable emotional moments.

61. What should I say to the widow, widower, or family of a deceased Service Member?

The very worst thing to do is to avoid a widow, widower, or family member because you're uncomfortable. Simple words of condolence are appropriate: "I'm very sorry for your loss." If you are friends, you can call and check on them, invite them out, or pay them a visit at a later time. Let them know you're there for them.

FLAG ETIQUETTE

62. What's the proper way to display the flag?

- The section of federal law dealing with American Flag etiquette is referred to as the Flag Code. The important thing to know is there are rules and expectations governing how the US flag should be displayed. Here are some basic guidelines, but you should also check the Flag Code (available on the internet) if you have questions.

- When the flag of the United States is displayed from a staff projecting horizontally or at an angle from the building, the union (the blue field) of the flag should be placed at the peak of the staff unless the flag is at half-staff.

- If not flown from a staff, the flag should be displayed flat, whether indoors or out. When displayed either horizontally or vertically against a wall, the union (the blue part) should be in the upper left when viewed.

- If you're hanging the flag in a window, the blue union should be in the upper left when viewed from the street

- The flag should be lighted at all times, either by sunlight or by an appropriate light source. Otherwise, it should be taken down prior to sunset.

- The flag should not be flown in rainy weather, unless the flag is designed for inclement weather use.

- The US flag should never touch the ground. Fold and store it properly and ceremonially.

- The flag should be cleaned and mended when necessary.

- When a flag is so worn it is no longer fit to serve as a symbol of our country, it should be destroyed by burning in a dignified manner. It is more respectful to take down a torn flag than it is to keep it flying. The proper disposal of the American flag is to burn it. The American Legion, Veterans of Foreign Wars, Disabled American Veterans Organizations, or a local Boy Scout or Girl Scout Troop often provide this service. The flag should never be thrown in the garbage.

- The flag of the United States of America should be at the center and at the highest point of the group when a number of flags of States are displayed from staffs.

- The flag should not be used for any decoration. Red, white, and blue bunting should be used, but never the flag. The blue stripe of the bunting should be on the top.

- Wearing the American flag as a cloth print is disrespectful. The wearing of an actual American Flag is considered improper in all circumstances. This includes draping it over oneself. The flag should not be used as part of a costume or athletic uniform, except the flag patch may be used on the uniform of military personnel, fire fighters, police officers, and members of patriotic organizations.

- The flag should never have any mark, insignia, letter, word, number, figure, or drawing of any kind placed on it, or attached to it.

- The flag should never be used for receiving, holding, carrying, or delivering anything.

63. When should the flag be displayed?

Section 6d of the Flag Code states the flag should be displayed on all days, but especially on the following days:

New Year's Day	Jan. 1
Inauguration Day	Jan. 20
Martin Luther King Jr.'s Birthday	3rd Monday in Jan.
Lincoln's Birthday	Feb. 12
Washington's Birthday	3rd Monday in Feb
Easter Sunday	(check your calendar)
Mother's Day	2nd Sunday in May
Armed Forces Day	3rd Saturday in May
Memorial Day (half-staff until noon, then full-staff until sunset)	last Monday in May
Flag Day	June 14
Father's Day	3rd Sunday in June
Independence Day	July 4
National Korean War Veterans Armistice Day	July 27
Labor Day	1st Monday in Sept.
Constitution Day	Sept. 17

Columbus Day	2nd Monday in Oct.
Navy Day	Oct. 27
Veterans Day	Nov. 11
Thanksgiving Day	4th Thursday in Nov.
Christmas Day	Dec. 25
Other days as proclaimed by the President of the United States	
The birthdays of States (date of admission) and on State holidays	

64. What is meant by half-staff and when is the flag displayed at half-staff?

"Half-staff" means lowering the flag to half the distance between the top and bottom of the staff. The flag is flown at half staff in mourning for designated principal government leaders and upon presidential or governor's order.

To place the flag at half staff, hoist it to the peak for an instant and lower it to a position half-way between the top and bottom of the staff. The flag is to be raised again to the peak for a moment before it is lowered.

Fly the flag at half-staff on the following days:

- Peace Officers Memorial Day (May 15); half-staff from sunrise to sunset.

- Memorial Day (Last Monday in May); half-staff until noon, and then full staff until sunset.

- Patriot Day (September 11); half-staff from sunrise to sunset.

- Start of Fire Prevention Week (First Sunday in October); half-staff from sunrise to sunset.

- National Pearl Harbor Remembrance Day (December 7); half-staff from sunrise to sunset.

- Upon reliable information that a past or present President, Vice-President, Chief Justice, or Speaker of the House has died.

- Upon Presidential proclamation or proclamation from your state's governor.

RESOURCES AND REFERENCES

Beam, Judy K. *Ruffles and Flourishes: A Guide to Customs & Courtesies of the Military.* Ohio: Daring Books, 1988. A concise newcomer's guide intended for Army wives.

Cline, Lydia Sloan. *Today's Military Wife: Meeting the Challenges of Service Life.* 6th ed. Pennsylvania: Stackpole Books, 2009. This in-depth and informative guidebook covers all aspects of military life from deployments, benefits, and budgeting to socials and protocol. It's intended for all branches and isn't service-specific.

Conetsco, Cherlynn and Anna Hart. *Service Etiquette,* 5th ed. Maryland: Naval Institute Press, 2009. In this comprehensive book, you'll find answers to almost any protocol/etiquette questions in military, professional, or diplomatic life. A great addition to your personal library.

Crossley, Ann and Carol A. Keller. *The Air Force Wife Handbook: A Complete Social Guide.* Florida: ABI Press, 1992. If you want a "just the facts" reference book, this is the one for you. It has lots of information about social events and life in the Air Force. Many of the "old school" traditions are introduced and explained here so you can understand them.

Crossley, Ann and Carol A. Keller. *The Army Wife Handbook: A Complete Social Guide.* 2nd ed. Florida: ABI Press, 2007. The Army counterpart to the above book. If you want a "just the facts" reference book, this is it. It has lots of information about social events and life in the Army. Many of the "old school" traditions are introduced and explained here so you can understand them.

Department of the Army. *Pamphlet 600–60: A Guide to Protocol and Etiquette for Official Entertainment.* Dec. 2001. Army specific guidance for official functions. Available online as a printable document.

Hickey, Robert. *Honor & Respect: The Official Guide to Names, Titles, and Forms of Address.* Washington: Protocol School of Washington, 2008. The go-to guide for information on forms of address for private citizens, professionals and academics, military personnel, diplomats, clergy, and officials, both US and international. This reference is available at your local library for clarification on specific titles and forms of address.

Leyva, Meredith. *Married_to the Military: A Survival Guide for Military Wives, Girlfriends, and Women in Uniform.* Revised and Updated. New York: Fireside, 2009. Besides having a chapter on protocol, this handy paperback will guide you through moves, finances, and health care with a chatty, girlfriend tone.

Long, Sheila M. *The Little Book of Etiquette: Tips on Socially Correct Dining.* New York: Barnes & Noble, 2000. This compact book with five chapters is a quick and convenient reference on table manners and how to be a gracious host/hostess.

McCaffree, Mary Jane and Pauline Innis. *Protocol: The Complete Handbook of Diplomatic, Official and Social Usage.* New Jersey: Prentice-Hall, 1977. The definitive book on proper protocol, to include information on order of precedence, titles and forms of address in written and oral communication, official entertaining, table seating arrangements, and flag etiquette.

Post, Peggy., et al. *Emily Post's Etiquette: Manners for a New World.* 18th ed. New York: Harper Collins, 2011. Investing in this book is an excellent idea. Although not military specific, it covers all manners-related dilemmas of modern life, including those involving mobile phones, email, and computers. Exceptionally readable and user-friendly.

United States Congress. *The United States Flag: Federal Law Relating to Display and Associated Questions.* Upd April 2008. Guidance on when, where, and how to display the US Flag. Available online by searching "US Flag Code."

ABOUT THE AUTHOR

Writing about military life comes naturally to Marna Ashburn Krajeski because she's seen it from all angles. She grew up an Air Force brat, served five years on active duty as an Army helicopter pilot, and was an Army wife for twenty years.

She's written two books about military family life--HOUSEHOLD BAGGAGE: THE MOVING LIFE OF A MILITARY WIFE (Wyatt-MacKenzie, 2006) and HOUSEHOLD BAGGAGE HANDLERS: 56 STORIES FROM THE HEARTS AND LIVES OF MILITARY WIVES (Wyatt-MacKenzie, 2008).

Marna attended the College of William and Mary in Virginia and earned her Master's degree in English at Austin Peay State University in Tennessee. Her articles and essays have been published in *Off Duty, Military Spouse, Married to the Military, American Baby, Skirt, The Military Times, SO Rhode Island, and the Providence Journal.* She's also the creator of GREAT GET-TOGETHERS and SMALL GET-TOGETHERS, party planning notebooks for all occasions, available at www.GreatGetTogethers.com.

Marna and her two nearly grown children live in Rhode Island, where they enjoy kayaking, surfing, and sailing.

Keep in touch with Marna at her website:
www.HouseholdBaggage.com.

Made in the USA
Middletown, DE
26 March 2022